MOUNTS VALLEYS
&
MYSELF

MOUNTS VALLEYS
&
MYSELF

Poems by
S.Vaidheeswaran

Translated by
Latha Ramakrishnan

Hawakal Publishers

Published by **Hawakal Publishers**
185, Kali Temple Road, Nimta, Calcutta 700049, India.

First edition: September, 2018

Printed and bound: S. P. Communications, Raja Dinendra
Chandra Street, Calcutta 700009.

Contact: Bitan Chakraborty (Founder, Hawakal)
Email: info@hawakal.com

Cover concept and design: Bitan Chakraborty

ISBN-13: 978-93-87883-32-1 (Paperback)

Price: INR Three hundred and Fifty only (Rs. 350/- only)

Dedicated to my mother

ACKNOWLEDGEMENTS

I wish to thank my young friend Mr. Rajesh Subramanian, a person with deep love for and knowledge of literature, and a literary translator, without whose active collaboration this book would not have been published.

I have always remained indebted to Mr. Ashokamitran (late), an eminent writer and my life long friend, whose foreword written for my earlier book still stands relevant and vibrant for reproducing this collection.

I wish to thank Ms. Latha Ramakrishnan, a poet and my translator, who has for many years shown keen interest in my poems and always has been enthusiastic in translating them for wider readership.

I wish to thank Dr. Kiriti Sengupta and Hawakal Publishers who showed active interest and concern to bring out this book so beautifully and professionally.

S. Vaidheeswaran

A WORLD OF INTRICATE METAPHORS

The very fact someone has been known to you for nearly fifty years makes it difficult for you to introduce him appropriately and with relevance to the situation. My interactions with Vaidheeswaran roughly are at least twenty years less, and by then he had been identified as one of the most important voices in the new poetry movement in Tamil. It was when he was bringing out his first collection of poems in the early 1970's that I had the occasion and also adequate material of his to get to know him as a poet, perhaps one of the most important poets in contemporary Tamil writing.

Even as early as 1961, Vaidheeswaran had employed a completely original idiom in his poetry. On the surface, his language seems a formal, literary language but, as one goes from line to line, reader will realize that the poet is unfolding a new world in a totally new pattern of words. Metaphors never had been utilized in Tamil so fluently, abundantly and tellingly as in Vaidheeswaran's creations. There is enough inwardness to make the poems intonate the inner voice but his poetry is almost of the external world, an extremely rich universe which is full of most surprising variety. The very lofty and the seemingly trivial get converted into a veritable magic of linguistic pattern, at the same time not being removed from human feeling. The most significant aspect is that the poet is never confessional, never self-pitying, never regretting, but always creates a well of concern and attention to the world around him.

The translator who has rendered Vaidheeswaran's poems for this volume is noted for her competence and sensitivity. How well she has rendered the poet's unique Tamil version and Tamil voice is a thing to be judged by readers from languages other than Tamil. I have always been apprehensive to visualize Vaidheeswaran's poetry in any other language mainly because his lines in Tamil are richly loaded as they are original and elusive. But he has attained great fame in translation in other Indian languages. This volume is a very special challenge and I do hope Vaidheeswaran's poems in English will delight poetry lovers as much as his originals have always delighted me.

Ashokamitran
Chennai

CONTENTS

Enigma

The Sun shines
irrespective of your liking or disliking.
Cannot stop the rain
though may strongly desire so.
Neither can the storm
be halted with a command to do so.

Only after an uproarious descent
does even a waterfall turn
into a subservient river.

These poems too seem to be of
same nature.
Enigmatic outpour of
an innate tenacity.

The Moon that has fallen into the well

Move down deep enough to lift up
The Moon that has fallen into the well.
Her body is fully wet;
Ensure she does not slip through your fingers.
Sweet scented is her body –
Lay it gently on the sands.
Full of light – shines her body
Cover it up with the reeds.

Beautifully flies her hair –
Comb it with the air that flows over her.
Let her wavering breasts be
Embraced fully by the soft vines.
Her face with shadows of an unknown fear –
Brighten it up by applying turmeric all over.
After doing all the above
Nurse her affectionately with warm poems.
Apply honey all over her body
And send her off on a
Safe journey to the edges of the sky.

Before the darkness ends
And before the death of the night,

Ward off the evils and send her back.
Before the mericiless demon
Who would wield his scorching heat to
torment her
Throw her off, safely on the sky.

Before the mischievous Krishna
Playfully kicks, taking her to be a
Well rounded ball,
Send off the golden moon.

Select the most apt moment and
Send her off through a path that is not cursed
by
Thundering rain, ghastly winds and
Deadly lightnings.

Make the gentle sky her protector
And the star that blinks without a moment's
rest, her friend.

In this world, apart from us who have
Seen her and heard about her
None else should come to know of this event.

Move down deep enough to lift up
The Moon that has fallen into the well.

A Sound Within

Age is a '*Lifometer*'
turning us into ants inside Time
moving us slowly
nurturing and torturing
it drags us along
into all too dark, directionless
jungle of events.
It depicts years as life.
Stirring and severing several images
making us believe them to be our own self,
pushes us headlong into
the valleys of middle age.
Rising up still, realizing
within ourselves the self-deception
when we falter
gives a walking-stick, it helps us
to climb ashore.
Unable to move on
standing on the road
where destiny had ceased
when we look back
Age seems not to have been
But as a dream lost without a trace.
I have no mouth to laugh.

The Dark Wisdom

Unable to stare at the flame
I ducked my face.
As an abandoned corpse, the shadow lay
stretched.
Is it me?
Or a cartoon of myself drawn on the soil?
That which is cleaves my eye -
Is it sarcasm? Gloom?
Or the norm?
Wearing as the front-row teeth
all those medals snatched at
thousands of beauty pageants
lying on the moon, the heart swelling with
pride -
on photographs in dozens
with all myriad shades of smiles?
But?
Why this dismal shadow for me?
No, this is not 'me' at all…
I don't have a shadow like this.
So on and so forth
wailing within,
and running nonstop -

but, what's the use?
The devil possessed never left.
Though the dress could be torn
what to do with the skin.
Burying the eye into the dark
with hands shivering
feeling acutely restive and screaming
when I tried looking
I had lost sight.

Do I have a self?
Where lies my shadow?
Pushing and crushing
Gloom was munching and consuming me.

God's Regret

With faith in trees
I created birds.
I did not think of humans at that time.

.

Apriori

Waves are not the ocean.
No ocean without the waves.

Why Sir?

Why sir, in public,
You never fail to utter that man's name.
All out of a fear.

Why, also, in public
You never mention this man's name?
All out of a sense of respect only.

Life

Dew, at grass blade's tip
A towering tree's just born leaf
A dash of mercy from the heart's depths
A lightning's forehead's warmth
Scattering seed dust.

Memories' reborn sperm
Clamour that hid itself from the intellect.
A deluge that swallowed the dam.

I, devoured by myself.
A honey born within myself
Poem's revelry.

Accident

In a momentary collapse
scattered all over with a deafening roar
the screams that explode out of mangled
body.

Getting buried inside the bloody slush
the faces turned charcoal balls and sobbed.
The rail tracks stood erect upon the sky
as broken giant bones.
Languages of diverse regions
Impacted by the same misery
turned wordless.

Wind alone was wailing
uncontrollably.

In the desolate valley.

Parting

Parting the tree
The flowers softly spread over the soil
Separating the sorrow silently
From death.

Ties

I have long forgotten
my kite that had
broken off from its string
in the open sky in the distant past.
Did not realize till today
that it has been
wagging its tail all along
on my home's terrace.

Above

Slender shadows
on the white wall.
Free exhibition
of the spider's artistry.

Attachment

The legs of houseflies
that quivered hungrily in the wind
on seeing a morsel of food
perforated it with pleasure..

the hand that rose to hit it -
it knows for sure -

yet
the morsel held it tight
till demise.

Pardon

Though the trees are destroyed
relentlessly
The koels have no anger
towards anyone.

Their voice still sing of love
directed at the 'human' yet to evolve.

Again and Again

Inside the wind
thoughts struggle
for a word.

Dumb heat
The sun throbs inside the water
with no opportune moment to come out.
Human fingers crush with no respite
the udders that don't secrete any milk.

Unable to drive off the mosquitoes
the man without fingers
lies bundled in the street-corner.

In one false step
occurrences with their totality lost
happen day after day.
Raging lunatics also
lie in wait after throwing bombs
that remain unexploded.
Some victories we don't need now.
Let animosities alone suffer defeat
Life would thrive then.

A Curse

At my feet
a cat remains in penance
praying to God
for the *idli* that would escape my fingers.
To make its penance
turn fruitful
I become a mini-god
letting the *idli* escape from my fingers.
Many a time I would turn into a
bizarre God
retaining the *idli* in my grip
would show only my thumb.
With its patience evaporated
a hell would gleam
in the semi-white half eyes of the cat.
with patience evaporated
a hell would gleam
in its semi-white eyes
Teeth would slightly sprout
at the tip of its claws
In the depths of the night
a scream would slice the darkness.
In the cat's throat

the blood of a rat would
gush forth.
Even after my death as a rat
inside my dream.
I would wake up in a jerk
with a throbbing heart
Not knowing why.

Midday

In the spread of silence
wave after waves
Koel's voice.

It cried
intermittently
into the absorbent ears.

At those instances when
Stepping further
and
the divergences
Went on crying
Weirdly within.

Separation

The kinship between you and I
is akin to the one
between the fire and the worm.
Let's concur and agree:

You light up my surroundings
though from a distance.
Let me graze the grass all around
and turn them into manure.

None is ruined
in a life so lived, right?

A Tale

Once upon a time, in a town, there was a
parrot. It had two wings. Its nose was curved
and red in colour. Its eyes always looked wide-
open, blinking like castor nuts.
It would always be whiling away the time
sitting on a low-hung branch, watching the
street.
None had seen it fluttering its wings or flying.

Yet, none doubted its identity as a parrot.

'That parrot is so beautiful.... But why is it so
inanimate?' asked one.

'True, it's beautiful.... But it is lifeless.
More or less the same as we are.
Merely existing as if full of life', I responded.

He was striving hard to comprehend.

Ignorance

The lone coconut tree
unaware of its height on earth
keeps banging against
the glassy sky
through the epochs.

Why?

A few drops hidden to the eyes
came into view once they soaked the soil.
That evening your eyes
as a little boy's watering mouth
on seeing sugar candy
drew and drenched me
in mid-rain!
With my hand kerchief I blocked the rain, at
once
But, it took a long time
for the memory to dry up.

Advaitha

With joy, sorrow blends as sugar
Light is always the scale of darkness.
Deep meditation of the glowing charcoals
that don't sway in the wind.
valley's abysses hold aloft
the mountain peaks.
The moment of you and I
two different ones
turning into one;
Hatred and love
losing their identities
merge in a tight embrace.
The moment the mouth opens saying
'Marvellous!'
Within the question that wonders
If it is so natural
Lies the answer
That is thriving already.

Loft

With trembling fingers,
blowing the dust
that had accumulated over the long years,
I unfolded a shrunken paper
to read it at dusk.
It's a poem written
to my ladylove.
The poem remains alive
still.

Twilight Zone

Memories
Fishes that slip through the fingers
A chameleon beyond our grip
that hides in the thicket of Time.
How do the names of faces get
mixed up?
Sometimes they displace the dead years
planting them somewhere else.
Times of the day
dawn in different order more often.
Events that took place yesterday
appear to be happening today;
The mind also believes
that things seen today
will happen only in the future.
Morn noon even night
dawn in different alignment
many a time.
So getting cheated it turns
the mind becomes confusion confounded.
A spider-web.
You who were familiar while entering
turninto an unknown face while leaving,

why so?
With memory-sacks scattering and spilling
Incidents roll down.
Weightless head.
Primary school without a teacher.
Now the sky pervades all through me.
Stepping out resolutely
Now I go strolling with an umbrella in hand
Is it walking- by no means.
When did the children turn into fish?
Is this pond's depths?
Or, a unique a crimson sky?
In my own journey
I cease to be!
My Room's Door

If I close it
standing outside
it bursts open.
On opening it from inside
it shuts at once.

Fearing the robber
I locked its mouth,
only to hear its strong shouts.
If wind were to touch it
it wails aloud.

I applied oil;
it moved apart.
Why? Asked I.

'For this life that moves in semi circles
what's the use of customary rituals;
leave me, let me fall'
Said the door.

One fine day
it stood parting fully from me.
Wonder, when I would let it part me.

Thirst

Untying the horse at sky's zenith
He came running to my door.
Like the dancing steam upon the boiling rice-pot
with a hot breath that proved restive
I woke up with my day-dream disrupted.
No time to ponder who you are.
"Thirst!..... Thirst!" leaned he
upon my shoulder.
"Bearing fire in my tongue
I wander like a dog.
West to East
I wander herding.
Thirst.... oh, how I crave water" -
So he writhed in agony.

The moisture springing in my heart didn't flow in
my hand.
Leaping and running as too light cotton
carrying a water-sprinkler
I tried burrowing the river's back.
Even my nail didn't get wet.
Inserting my leg into the newly dug well

I rose and came out as a blister.

All over the barren land
the 'routine' betraying me,
the seed that I had sown yesterday
revealed itself in my heart.
I who had sown asked
"No water, but do you have honey?
No time to wait" said I.
'Proper time should come
for impregnating and springing.
Come, let's see."
-so the seedling bent.

Alas, the Time.
Thirst knows no season.
What would I say to the scarred mouth
that awaits at my doorstep.
What land is this...
My heart and body
Melt and turn into salt;
With eyes swelling,
carrying the bucket with an empty hand
I rushed to my doorstep.

'Please wait for half-a-second' said I.
'Oh no! I'm God. Time is not for me.
Also, if I bear with it any more
the horse getting unleashed
would swallow the ends of the sky -

You too have turned so sticky with sweat
So saying, with sweat wiping his forehead
He fluttered spreading his wings.

'Thirsty…. I feel thirsty!'
So I pursued involuntarily.
"Ah yes. Thirst _ You gave no water!
But I've given thirst.
Hail it and sing!" said he and flew into the Sky.
The cloud neighed.

Selfless Love

Flashing as a fire
the lightning disappears
into the dark instantly.
Your smile, when you walk past me
is no different.
Often, in the evening
I long that the rain should pour only for me.
Selfless love still eludes me.
Till I attain it, my dear,
do not turn me into an orphan.

A Question

How a dotty insect
with legs sprouted
all over its body
would copulate
is my cranky question.

But on the land wherever
you see waves after waves of
dotty insects -
proving the query redundant.

Tongues

Despite having tongues
like snakes
the waves never
bite the leg.

Hissing softly
tickling you more and more
it hauls away the sand
from beneath the feet
like the mischievous pranks of
the mean people.

On Fire

Rocks .
wherever I turned
rocks.
From a tiny hole
sprouts with full force
a small plant.
All at once Life
became easy.

Up Above on a Day

All around, soap-foam clouds.
Widespread white woodlands.
In the vacuum that fills in
a patch of sky
that simulates bluish lakes.
one drop of sky
simulating bluish lakes!
Down under heaps of
buildings criss-cross
as teeth sprouting from the soil.
While flying high
towns turn nameless.
The heart that roams inside the plane
rejoices in two ways.
On my right -the galactic grandeur.
On my left, a baby face
that touches my finger and smiles
mischievously.

Differences

Going round and round
the tree
so friendly
the butterflies
touching each and every
blossom
enquiring after their
well-being.

Piercing through the
dusts
the rays of the
faraway Sun
leap, sloping as
sky-goads
so concerned about
global cleanliness.

Little drops of sky
flows amazed underneath
my feet.

Many an unusual flower

bloomed of tree entering
tree
stand so close to
each other in harmony
sharing the water of
the same root.

A cow so gullible
As not knowing alien from kin
licks so affectionately and
feeds with its milk
the hapless calf standing in the
middle of the street
not knowing who its mother is.

It is in the same street
the father beats his son with a cane....
"Will you dare befriend the boy next street?
Will you?
Will you?"

Somehow

Tender fingers folded by someone.
The tiny flower buds
that extend an invitation to open them
with their radiating fragrance.
I do find a lot many of them
In the early morning.

The very same buds
as bursting little dawns
unfolding and smiling
never escape my eyes.

Yet, how secretively Time
retains within itself
the tiny little moments
a bud blossoms
into a flower.

Squirrel

The crows scatter and disperse
Only to regroup and scatter,
making the sky bluer to me.

The rhythm of the flowers that bloom
like colourful fireworks,
only to wilt and fall,
makes the tree enlarge as a green sky
In my half eye.

The coconut tree
inspite of the countless heads that crown it
stands thoughtless
makes me think deep within.

The squirrel playfully trolls up and down on it
like thoughts often do;
I stand powerless to act.
Looks as if
like the mind to me , the tree is to the squirrel,
to keep playing tirelessly.

Today

These black birds
that fly with their
feathers bursting,
between the sea and the sky-
are they the city's morning smile?

These cloud children
that move with a speed
to their school up above-
halt hither and thither
with a hesitation-
In search of which mother's face?

Inspite of dawn's birth
the moon that continues
its sleep shamelessly in the spatial mattress-
What day dream could be behind?

In the mind's eye that
expanded for no reason
fell some images on their own-
Are they really the reality?

Flight 2

This shadow that comes
chasing while I fly
frightens me forever.

If I contain the shadow
inside my wings
and remain without flight,
hunger flays me mercilessly.

At night ,
the shadow could be locked
Inside the night
preventing it from pursuing me.
.

But the night fruit
that is visible at the heights
seems not suited to appease my
hunger.

Many a time
with hunger scorching the shadow,
shedding off fear itself
turns into my flight,
becoming a second name for
Livelihood.
.

Situations

Time and again
peeping at the darkness
outside the doors,
with dry eyes
and patience gone dry,
she kept tearing off the garland
mitigating the anguish of her fingers.

He, fallen on the ground somewhere
near the shop, as an orphaned dog.
Flows throughout the night
the gutter, garrulously.

The Wait

Beyond the window
Night's wait so high.
There hang slices of sky
at the mouth-corners of
wild cloud beasts.

To have little bites en route
stars in clusters.
A curved crescent moon
serves as a side dish.

There's no way other
than taking in the stride
The sorrows that strike
without any reason.

None would have expected
a creation blown large
Only with air and water
Would encroach the whole sky.

Intention's intensity
gets diluted in execution.

The procession of the vehement clouds
continues ceaselessly
blocking the window thoroughly.

I wait in vain throughout the night
for a clear sky
Like a passenger on the window seat
gasping for breath.

Awakening 2

Half asleep
lying in the cot,
with dreams that had not vanished
I looked at the sky.

In the space that had not seen the dawn,
it floats
like a wading bird without fluttering its wings.
givingup itself fully to the gentle wind all
around.

I awoke.

Torment

In the bicycle
stolen from me twenty years back
He still continues to ride
Without realizing
That I knew the truth.

Going back and forth crossing me,
For years, since then,
Without remorse,
With a smile on his face always.

Memories of his crime
Fully wiped out of my mind
Both of us talk to each other
Out of habit.

Yesterday, spotting him walking unsteadily
and without the cycle,
I enquired if he was well.

Holding his hand across his chest
He said
' The air does not hold nowadays;

Chokes and gasps often;
Don't know how many more days
Will manage to keep moving;
At times makes me think
If it does not belong to me'.

' The body... or the cycle..?
What tormented him now...?'
I remain confused.

Vision

'A hanging suspended ball
playing in the world'.
The poets of the bygone eras
of the enchantress of Science
who has asked to tell tales for feeding
assembling
and hauling the heart upwards
Today at dawn
a pair of new eyes
scanning the sky
through the kitchenette window
finding the ever-silver moon
drank coffee.

Address

Indeed blasphemy, sacrilegious
-scribbling the street-address of the saint
at the backside of a
harlot's picture.

Going beyond, walking ahead
stumbling in the dark
in the East
between the temple-car shed and the shrine
searching in futile for the door that opens
and at last
thinking if a ripe body is tapped
the path would unfold on its own
and then
growing apprehensive
that if a saint is rolled over
the harlot would laugh
to her heart's content
I stood there as a rooster
and crowed
right in the middle of the street,
yesterday.

Advice

"Smoke not"
So my grandpa saying to my dad
my son too learnt from me.
True indeed.
(But) that which all of us relish
is of very high quality.
My grandson bears testimony!

Conflict

Between
Yesterday and Tomorrow
we stand
and suffer
Today.

With Time's invisible
burden
the neck broken
and the heart worn-out.
Inside dreamless life
we've turned nightless day
Today.

Oh, why did the long-eye bird flew off
without halting ?
Upon moon's fair countenance
saw we
machine's smoke-coating.
The loan-calculation
on the mud wall
stars shown.
To fly, there is wind

There is Time to go past….
In the fear-filled heart-cage
flutters so anguished
the crippled life.

Between Yesterday and Tomorrow
We stand and suffer.
Innumerable are
the catamarans that pull to the shore
the heart that dreams to
keep swimming sans Time…..
To stand with nil thought,
if paused
"What time is it?" asks the world.

Inside the roar of
the tiger called hunger
green parrots turned dumb.
The aged parrots of the branch
bend inside burrow.

With tomorrow's fragrance and
the stench of yesterday
In confusion incomprehensible
the heart sways
and blabbers day after day
in dumb sleep
caught between Yesterday and Tomorrow.

Marina Beach

Seashore.
Upon the sand
the people - a
moving bridge.

Intermittently – as
child's eye
astonishing
the sight of lights
In myriad hues and shades.

In the dark
in numerous postures
building dream in heart
and dispersing the
sand
playful youth.

There
several 'lonely' feet.
Yearning
and going in search of
merciful moisture

and press hard
upon the rim of wave
the smell of fish
pervading
and the usual audio of
the radio
prove salt to Life.

People are a
moving bridge.

Dictionary

'What is Ahimsa?' asked
my child.

The meaning read long ago
has escaped my memory.
Same is the case with
myneighbour.

They looked at me
amused with the thought
whether such a word
exists at all in the
world at large.

The meaning for that word
would surely be found in
old dictionary - thought I
and dusting it looked into the volume.

Thank god - the dictionary still remained
As eroded map.

I tried to unfold the

'D' page......
It all stuck together
As matted hair.
Only after intense struggle
I could succeed.

Still, a hole in the 'D'
Dart, dear, Do, Day, Dawn, Drum
- Everything had
Suffered holes.

Non-violence losing 'non'
Remained all violence.

Should discard the dictionary.
Nothing else can be done. Or,
can give it to the date-fruits' vendor
and get date-fruits in return.

Felt ashamed to concede to my son
the fact that I have forgotten it.....
Interpreting it wrongly would be
doing wrong to one whole generation....

'My dear son, though knowing
I'm unable to prove it to you
as things stand today.

Bring it alive, finding out its meaning
in your own way.

But, don't lose it
as we've done....' Observed I.

This was all I could say.

What to say?

1.

When I think of God
tears swell in my eyes.

When I think of religions
'Oh God', my heart boils.

2.

Incessantly swinging my
hands and floating in
the sea of sorrow
has become a routine for me.

But just a tiny speck of joy
drowns me.

3.

This time that wagon
escaped in a hairline of a second
from killing me....
Shivering I looked back.
It goes past
hope-filled,
but still so fast.

Cockroach

It was dead
I thought…..
But, it moves!

Though felt relieved for a moment
to see a life saved
the next instant
a sense of derision
so unbecoming of my intelligence:

'That vendor has cheated me –
has sold me 'adulterated' thing.
Next time should be careful to buy the pesticide
taking care to ascertain the *Agmark* symbol -
so that henceforth cockroaches deceive me not
as deceased'.

Gift

Seeing him coming close
taking him to be a known face
smiled I
so friendly.

In response
he too smiled
being civilized.

Only after he went past
I realized that he is not someone
known to me.

Still,
the fact that I could
treat a stranger with love
is indeed a good start,
'by mistake' notwithstanding.

Silence

Sound's slumber
Lives' primal darkness.
Unparted lips of a talk.
Memory's iceberg.
Discourse of enlightened souls.
Love's signal.
Soft music's pollen dust.
Words' resting stone.

The virgin membrane of Time
is stamped and torn
by the city's daily delirious run—
Silence.

Ruin

Civilization abducted forests.

In the ash flood cemetery spread
died silently the trees smashed.
For the generations that have
erected houses in all arrogance
no sky to borrow wind.

All too often, as the prick of conscience
quicker all over the land.
Beating with their hands, the
countenance sans vision
our lineage keeps on
digging and searching for the
seeds lost
in vain.

Flowery Feet

In the flowerless tar roads
the feet turn flowers to the eyes.
In the street sea with speeding cars
the feet turn into floating flowers.

In the sun-scorching
bare floor, on the way facing you
come hesitantly the white rabbits
under the shade of a long skirt.

Stamping the soil,
Unsettling the heart,
Moved ahead
Mocking at the flowers-
The feet.

The Spring

As a slice of sky
ever on the move
between two flying crows -
an uncoloured mind
with broken boundaries
and frontiers torn apart-
widening in its length
and lengthening in width
while trying to enfold things all around.

In the marvelous state
when a moon caught in between
a few moments
shines glowing radiantly,
Life turns so very pleasant
and sets out afresh.
Sing in praise!

The Magnanimous Sun

Long walk
scorching Sun
en route
emboldened by a tree's shade
I halted, cursing
the sun to be damned.

When I looked above
tantalized by a mesmerizing voice
that pulled my attention over the tree-
looking for a koel;
The very same sun
winked at me beautifully.

My face blushed in red.

Doghood

That dog
is a real good dog.
Astonishingly never had it
a mouthful of shit
even by mistake.

The urge to gobble meat
bathing in the gutter
-the habit of the beggarly street-dog
to fight for the castaway residual dishes
stayed away from it
since birth.

It is an exception
to the idiotic convention
of going round feet alien -
wagging the tail again and again.

Not turning ungrateful
for some meager eatable –
with approach so righteous…..

In essence
it stayed well above
dog-sense.
To put it in a nutshell–
it is incorrect to call it
Animal.

Hark!
It has so civilized a bark!

Even when confronting robbers
without touching them it would
care the lot
in a respectful manner;
-what a grand demeanour!

One day
with legs and body
writhing and twisting
it lay there
at the street corner
on the throes of death.

Seeing
a dog of the adjacent household
so uncouth
drew closer
sympathizing
and licking it and cooling it
with its shit-filled mouth

observed,

'Don't you feel sad, my friend...
The cleanliness you possessed
so unsuited to the life of a dog
doesn't seem to be bad.

Yet, today you're lying here
worm-infected, ailing
afflicted with unwarranted pain
and wailing
which I, a weakling
can in no way justify at all.

Yet, I have this to say.
Please - in death's desperate haste
don't you go away
cursing your life as a mere waste.

Wait a little...
Wait a little....'

So the street dog went on howling
non-stop.

The Train and the Window

With sorrow brimming in the eyes
lips quivering like the grass-blades,
in the heart-pond
word-frogs so weak, slipping
and the meaning turns obscure,
your sublime countenance
wailed within me
the pain of parting.

I ,
holding the train,
sending countless kisses in the wind
tried to caress your heart
in vain.

Thoughts as ants,
carrying to and fro, up and down
incidents innumerable and panting
turned the heart into a disturbed beehive.
With love-string tightening by the moment
drawing closer together,
you and me.
Or, the train whistling hard

dragged you with a harsh pull.
I turned terribly restive.

With the window moving ,
the eyes, face and hands
turning wet,
as the window moved on and on......
another face and another anguish surfacing,
the windows moving and disappearing,
another face and longing
as a lightning flash
appearing disappearing appearing,
as tragic pictures dried up in the air
hundreds of faces, hands, jerks, cries....
All borne by the hurrying windows
terrified my eyes.

The crowds and shouts merging
the scene's moisture stuck in my eyes,
I saw the steam-smoke flying up above.
In the momentary delusion of my mind
parting and courting turned into a shared
emotion.

Life and body
expanded as the world.
Train and window disappearing
as un-real.
Sorrow stood as the window of Love.

Sneeze

In the corner, untying the evening plaits
sank the sun.
In the interim hanging suspended space
of jasmine creeper
as a seer sans attachment
swirling came a tiny insect.
Wonder-struck when I drew closer
the nose caught in the web.
In the sneeze that grabbed the nose
Art turned unleashed.

Benevolence

When the shadows of birds
blended with that of the tree on the ground
the branches fluttered still more;
Beneath,
little specs of light
opened their mouths wide.
A few fruits fell on the
ground silently.
The mind wondered if
it was a fruit or benevolence.

Right

In the sewage drain of his household
neighbour's dog lying and rolling
became habitual.
Though he chased it out
asserting his right with all his might,
it refused to budge.
One day, he hit it with a stick round and tall
filled to the brim with anger.
Barking in pain, with tail curled
the dog leapt out and ran
The sewer water splashed and
fell into his mouth.
His house's sewage.

Shadowy Leaf

The leaves fallen into the water
dance like delicate fingers
Inviting me tantalizingly.
Not knowing
how to evade the shadow
and pluck the leaf,
I turn into a stork
and stand in water
in the mid-day.

A Parrot Within

Late evening
a caged parrot inside the bus
watches with concern
my face that hangs in my hands.

Like oil that spreads on the floor-
The noon's shadow spreads devoid of life.
Anticipating the grain
that would be fed with no certainty,
The parrot that would pick
fortune cards for one and all
jumps in joy
at seeing me hanging inside the bus.

Falling into the pits on the roads
Enraged, seething with anger
Holding the leather straps
Heads banging against the side rails
The parrot and I
share a common sorrow
The realization of which
brings forth a joy.

At times we curse each other
At other moments
we bond in friendship

Day after day
throughout the night
dreams to fly
would be born inside
the parrot, with broken wings.

Inside the blanket
my heart would be searching the
lost dreams
untiringly till dawn.

Voice

Like tin-bowls dragged along the floor
graze against night-walls-
-he voices of nightly beggars.

Bodies that don't have even shadows to cling to;
aimless lances hanging at the wall-corners,
being thrown into the dark.

Children inside the house with mouthful of food
would look frightened at the dark doorway -
with their fingers scratching the fear.
Bitter response gulped by the mother
would shut the door and bring inside the voice, pushing i

Yonder, the voice…. would still be
stuck to the street-corner.

Some morsels being unreachable
would be sticking onto the skies.

Verdict

The little ant didn't bite you;
Then why did you kill it?

It creeps playfully on your fenceless body-
Should your finger demand the ant's life
to be sacrificed?

Even if bit by it
you wouldn't fall dead.
Yet why crush the ant?

Does the silent end of life of that dying ant
tell your crushing heart
that you did nothing wrong.

Killing an ant is probably
the easiest thing in this world.
Should you engage in its killing
just because it is so.

The Wait 2

In the street corner's garbage heap
a crushed crow lies dead
as a copy of death.

Scorching heat.
The black road melts and flows.
Therein stands a bus stand
as a skeleton bent and burnt.
A long wait-
With pain shooting through the knees,
turning the legs numb and wooden.
The bus has not arrived yet.

A mid-day.
One strong swirl of wind
that knocks off a thousand leaves dead.
A sudden attack of
mysterious spears launched
by the only *Yama* from up above.

In the small bonfire lit in front,
the rubbers that burn in it
and the orphaned old man
sing songs that loudly lament death.
We still wait for a bus
on this earth.

*Yama- God of death

92

Transfer

"Good Morning" said the nurse,
to wake up the patient in the morning.
The latter, getting up seething said,
"Madam, it was of course I
who gulped the capsule you gave me
to sleep.
But, somehow changing place,
instead of me ,
it was the capsule that slept!
Please do wake it up first".

Reason

He doesn't smile at me
these days
as he used to do.

Which word that I had
spoken to him last
could be the reason for this
I felt at a loss for four days.

He gleefully smiled at me today saying
'Now I have got that tooth removed'
I felt sad.

ABOUT THE TRANSLATOR

Latha Ramakrishnan is a Post-Graduate in English from Presidency College, Chennai. Poet, short-story writer, critic and translator, she writes poems under the pseudonym 'Rishi,' and short-stories under the pseudonym 'Anamika.' She has been associated with the Tamil Little Magazine circle for the past twenty-five years. Her works have been published in all Tamil little magazines. So far three short-story collections and ten poetry-collections, three books of essays on the poem-collections of fellow-poets, and more than thirty works of translation have been published. She translates from English to Tamil and Tamil to English. She regularly translates Modern Tamil poets into English and translates short-stories too.

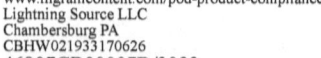